Excellent!
©Disney

Perfect work!
©Disney

Y... st...
©Disney

...done!
©Disney

Magical effort!
©Disney

I love to read!
©Disney

Let's practise!
©Disney

Let's have fun!
©Disney

Well done!
©Disney

You deserve a reward!
©Disney

Excellent!
©Disney

Good effort!
©Disney

Reading is fun!
©Disney

Take your time
©Disney

Well done!
©Disney

A sparkling effort!
©Disney

Good work!
©Disney

I love to read!
©Disney

Word perfect!
©Disney

Let's have fun!
©Disney

Well done!
©Disney

You deserve a reward!
©Disney

Great reading!
©Disney

Good effort!
©Disney

STEPS TO READING

Dear Parent:

Congratulations! Your child is taking the first steps on an exciting journey. **The destination? Independent reading!**

STEPS TO READING will help your child get there. The programme offers three steps to reading success. Each step includes fun stories and colourful art, and the result is a complete literacy programme with something for every child.

Learning to Read, Step by Step!

(1) **Start to Read   Nursery – Preschool**
• **big type and easy words** • **rhyme and rhythm** • **picture clues**
For children who know the alphabet and are eager to begin reading.

(2) **Let's read together   Preschool – Year 1**
• **basic vocabulary** • **short sentences** • **simple stories**
For children who recognise familiar words and sound out new words with help.

(3) **I can read by myself   Years 1-3**
• **engaging characters** • **easy-to-follow plots** • **popular topics**
For children who are ready to read on their own.

STEPS TO READING is designed to give every child a successful reading experience. The year levels are only guides. Children can progress through the steps at their own speed, developing confidence in their reading, no matter what their year.

Remember, a lifetime love of reading starts with a single step!

By Melissa Lagonegro
Illustrated by Pulsar Estudio

This edition published by Parragon in 2011

Parragon
Queen Street House
4 Queen Street
Bath BA1 1HE, UK

ISBN 978-1-4454-2112-4

Printed in Malaysia

A Dream for a Princess

PaRRagon

Bath · New York · Singapore · Hong Kong · Cologne · Delhi
Melbourne · Amsterdam · Johannesburg · Auckland · Shenzhen

There once was a girl
named Cinderella.
She was kind and gentle.

Cinderella lived with
her wicked Stepmother
and stepsisters.

She had many chores.

She served them tea.

She cooked their food.

She washed their clothes.

"Get my scarf!"
yelled one sister.
"Fix my dress!"
shouted the other.

They were very mean
to poor Cinderella.

One day,
a letter came
from the palace.
"Come meet the Prince
at a Royal Ball," it said.

The stepsisters
were very excited.
Cinderella was, too!

Cinderella dreamed of
wearing a fancy gown . . .

. . . and dancing with
the Prince.

Cinderella's Stepmother
gave her more chores.
Cinderella did not
have time to make
her ball gown.

"Surprise!"

cried her little friends.

They had made her

a fancy gown.

"Now I can go
to the ball!"
cheered Cinderella.

Oh, no!

The stepsisters

tore her gown.

It was ruined!

Piff, puff, poof!
Her Fairy Godmother
appeared.

"You cannot go
to the ball
like that," she said.

She waved

her magic wand.

Poof!

A royal coach.

White horses.

Two coachmen.

And a beautiful gown!

Cinderella was headed
to the ball!

At the ball,
the Prince saw
Cinderella.

"May I have this dance?" he asked.

They danced . . .

. . . and danced . . .

. . . and danced.

Cinderella was so happy.

She was wearing

a fancy gown.

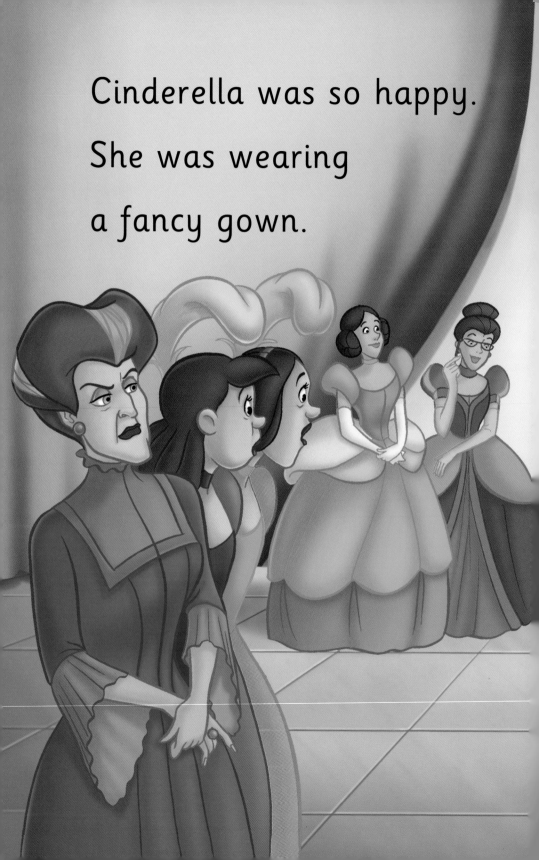

And she was dancing
with the Prince!

Her dream had come true!

Now turn
over for the
next story...

By Jennifer Liberts Weinberg
Illustrated by Peter Emslie and Elisa Marrucchi

Surprise for a Princess

PaRragon

Bath • New York • Singapore • Hong Kong • Cologne • Delhi
Melbourne • Amsterdam • Johannesburg • Auckland • Shenzhen

Once upon a time
there was a girl
named Briar Rose.

She lived in
the forest with
three fairies.
Their names were
Flora, Fauna
and Merryweather.

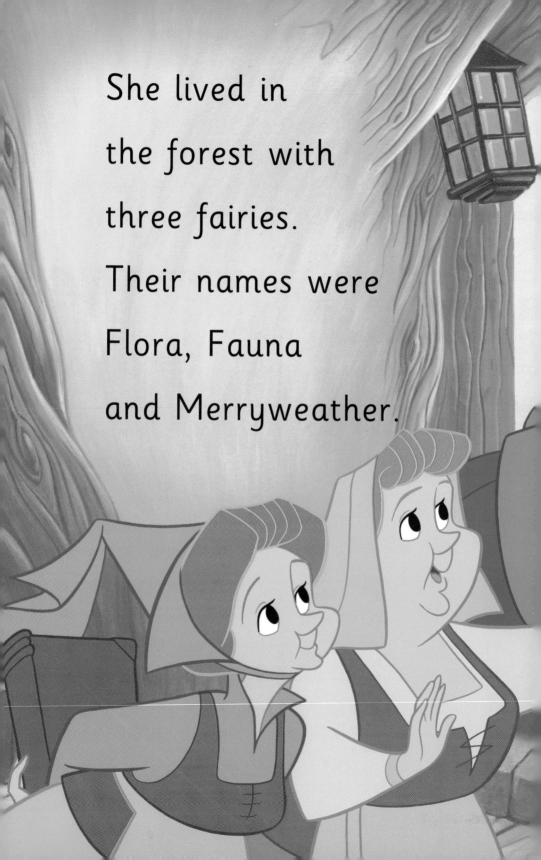

One day,
the fairies sent
Briar Rose out
to pick berries.

While she was gone,
they planned
a surprise.

"Let's have a party
for Briar Rose,"
said Merryweather.
"With a cake!"
said Fauna.

"And a dress
fit for a princess,"
said Flora.

Flora began

to make the dress.

She cut.

She pinned.

She trimmed.

Merryweather tried
to help.
But the dress
was a mess.

47

There was too
much cloth.
And there were too
many bows.

"Oh, no!"
said Fauna.
"It is awful!"
said Merryweather.

Fauna began
to make the cake.
She read from
a cookbook.
It said she needed
eggs, flour
and milk.

Fauna mixed.
And spilled.

And dribbled.
And dropped.

The milk dripped
onto the floor.
And the eggs
rolled off the table!
Crack!

At last the cake
was baked and iced.
But the icing slid
off the top.
And the candles
would not stand up.

"It is awful!"
said Merryweather.
"A flop!"
said Flora.

The fairies began
to worry.
Briar Rose was
coming home soon.

"I know just
the trick,"
said Merryweather.

She gave each fairy
a wand.
"Magic!"
they cried.
With a wave
of their wands . . .

Poof!
The cottage
was clean as
a whistle.

<u>Poof</u>!

The cake

was as pretty

as a picture.

Poof!
The dress
was fit
for a princess.

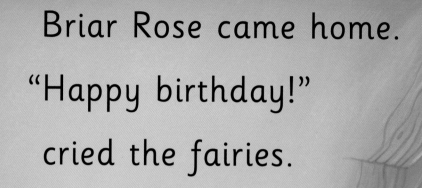

Briar Rose came home.
"Happy birthday!"
cried the fairies.

"Thank you!"
said Briar Rose.
"This is the
best surprise ever!"